Shipping Container Homes

A Complete Guide to Planning, Designing, and Building A Shipping Container Home

Table of Contents

Introduction 1

Chapter 1: What Are Shipping Container Homes? 3

Chapter 2: Benefits of Shipping Container Homes 12

Chapter 3: Overview of the Building Process 20

Chapter 4: Permits Needed for Building a Container Home ... 29

Chapter 5: How to Plan for a Container Home Build 41

Chapter 6: How to Source a Shipping Container 46

Chapter 7: How to Manage a Container Home Build 53

Chapter 8: Unique Design Ideas 58

Conclusion 62

Introduction

For many, owning a home is the ultimate goal in their life. To have a place that reflects who one is, their values, and that they can call their own is a natural dream to have. However, in today's economy, owning a house can be more difficult and unattainable than ever before, which has led many people to look at alternative means of home ownership, such as the shipping container home.

Growing in popularity in recent years, shipping container homes are attractive for a number of reasons. The most obvious is that they are environmentally friendly and a great alternative to building a brand-new home. It is entirely possible to build a shipping container home out of recycled containers, reducing the amount of waste in the waste stream, and providing quality building materials for a fraction of the price.

There are a lot of other reasons that container homes are gaining popularity, aside from their obvious environmental benefits. A shipping container home allows for a level of creativity in design that isn't possible with a traditional home. Shipping containers are designed to be locked together during transport, which allows you to imagine a home design in much the same way as you would approach building a Lego creation.

A shipping container home is also a more affordable option for home ownership as you can build new construction for far less than it costs to build a conventional home. They require fewer materials to build, and the materials are often much cheaper to begin with than those used in a traditional home. A shipping container home can also be built much faster than regular home construction, letting you see your vision through in as little as a couple of months.

A less well-known benefit is the potential portability of shipping container homes. It shouldn't come as much of a surprise when thinking about it since shipping containers are designed for, well, shipping. This means that these are very mobile dwellings that can be built offsite and then installed or even moved to a new location if desired.

In this book, we will touch on the basics of shipping container homes, the building process, and everything you will need to know to get started on your own shipping container home. Let's get started!

Chapter 1: What Are Shipping Container Homes?

The short answer to this question is that they are homes made out of shipping containers, but this is pretty obvious from their name. These are versatile constructions that can be as small or large as you wish them to be and can be configured in a wide range of ways to meet your needs, expectations, and aesthetic preferences. They are affordable to construct and can be built in a much shorter amount of time than traditional home construction.

However, just like with any type of construction, there are some things you will need to keep in mind and considerations that will need to be addressed so you end up with a home that meets your needs. These homes can be built in almost any shape and size, but they will still need to be structurally sound, and there are several important aspects to consider if you want this type of home.

The Basics

There are two standard sizes of shipping containers, which is part of what makes them so uniquely customizable. They come in 20 x 8 or 40 x 8, which provides for 160 square feet of living space and 320 square feet, respectively. They are also available in two different heights. Standard containers are 8.5 feet tall, and high cube containers are 9.5 feet tall. Though you can build with either, many prefer the high cube container as it provides for more headroom and vertical space, but the choice is yours.

These containers have been repurposed into a variety of structures, from market stalls to an extra office space in the backyard, so there is a long history of using these for a range of different types of construction.

The first-ever patent for a shipping container home was issued to Philip C. Clark on November 23, 1987. The US military also issued a report on the use of shipping containers for alternative uses back in 1977. The containers were used to transport and shelter prisoners during the Gulf War in 1991. This shows that they have a long and storied history, but their use in domestic contexts is a relatively recent phenomenon.

Shipping containers can be purchased new or used. They are made from high-quality steel and are largely produced in China. You can purchase shipping containers, new or used, with the choice depending upon your needs and budget. You will need to be diligent when purchasing a used container to ensure that it is in suitable condition. However, they are a lot cheaper than buying brand new containers, which can cost anywhere between $1,000-6,000, depending on the size and quality of the container.

There are estimates that there are as many as 14 million shipping containers that are currently not being used, making this an abundant building material that is simply collecting proverbial dust somewhere. As people have gotten more environmentally conscious, they are looking at areas of the waste stream where material can be removed and used for other purposes, and the shipping container is an excellent candidate.

Shipping containers are designed for a very specific purpose: to transport large loads of material to far off places around the world. However, once they have served their purpose, they are often disposed of even though the container is still structurally sound and in good repair.

There are national, local, and even online dealers that sell shipping containers. Shopping online is convenient and can be a good first step when trying to source shipping containers, but it isn't recommended to make the entire purchase exclusively online. It really is best that you physically see the containers before purchase if at all possible, particularly if you are buying a used container. A national seller may deliver for a fee, but local sellers often don't, which is why their prices tend to be lower.

You will want to take this into consideration when deciding where to buy your containers from. For many people, it is worth the extra cost to have the containers delivered as it is one less thing they have to concern themselves with. However, if you have access to the right equipment, this isn't going to be an issue. Smaller, standard-sized containers can often be transported with a forklift and a regular truck. The larger 40-foot containers may require a crane to move, however.

Since they are built to carry heavy loads and travel thousands of miles, shipping containers are incredibly sturdy and tough. They are designed to withstand the elements and are resistant to wind, water, and even things like salt damage.

You can combine different sizes of containers and stack multiple ones together for a multi-floor design. You can remove walls from containers, cut them in half, and create a completely unique floor plan that is unlike anything you can build with regular materials. Many people work with engineers and architects to create their own personalized design, but there are also a growing number of companies that sell prefabricated shipping container homes in a range of different floor plans.

Being modular in design makes them very versatile when it comes to creating different floor plans or configurations. They are designed to interlock with other containers for safety during transport, which makes combining multiple containers for a larger living space incredibly easy and very secure. This interlocking nature can actually enhance the strength of the structure.

Some people make tiny homes from just one or two containers, whereas others are absolutely massive. There are even shipping container constructions that have been cladded with traditional housing materials, making them indistinguishable from regular homes or buildings from the outside. As people have gotten more daring and creative with designs, these homes have continued to grow in popularity.

This type of home is pretty popular among the eco-friendly segment of the population as it allows you to build a home predominately out of recycled materials. When built well, these can be incredibly efficient homes and are conducive to an off-the-grid lifestyle.

Unique Considerations

The shipping industry is a huge and varied enterprise, and shipping containers are made for a variety of functions and thus to different levels of quality in design. It is important to know that certain containers that are used to ship things like noxious materials aren't recommended for use in home construction. If you plan on using used shipping containers, you will need to do a little homework to find out their origins.

Containers are meant to take a beating. They must be built to withstand over the road trucking as well as overseas shipping, which means they are well-built and durable, often resistant to wind and water. Regardless of the type of container you choose, you will not want to purchase them sight unseen. You need to see them in person so you can gauge their level of quality and how well they have been maintained.

There are what are called one-way containers that are, as the name implies, not meant for multiple shipments and are thus not built of as high-quality materials as other containers. These are not suitable for use in building a shipping container home as they aren't designed for longevity and are made from substandard materials.

Some used containers will be sold "as is," which means they may not be in good repair and that they could have been used in the transport of hazardous materials, which can damage the container and make them unsuitable for further use. For this reason, it is not recommended that you use "as is" containers in the construction of your home.

This is a novel type of home design that, while not new, is only recently starting to grow in popularity to a point where cities and state governments are addressing their unique needs. This means that you will need to look into local and state building and zoning regulations to ensure that it is legal to build a shipping container home in your area. You will also need to research what standards it will have to meet in order to pass an inspection. This will all vary from area to area.

This is really one of the most frustrating aspects of shipping container homes - laws and regulations often haven't had time to catch up with these new methods of construction, which can make for some headaches in getting all the proper permits. A shipping container home, like any other residential construction, will need to meet certain codes and standards for occupancy.

It should be noted that there are states and areas where the construction of this type of home is prohibited, so this will be one of the first things you need to investigate. You are more likely to have an easier time getting the right permits and permissions in more rural or remote areas. Urban areas tend to have less space for new construction to begin with, and also have much more stringent rules and regulations.

A shipping container is rather narrow, which can mean you will need to rethink how you use the space in this type of home. You also have the option of removing one or more walls so as to create a wider, more open floor plan.

It is important to note that while this can be a very affordable way to build a home, it isn't always the cheapest, depending on your design. A complex, larger design will, like any construction, cost more to build, and with the unique nature of shipping containers, some complex designs may even cost more to build than a traditional home. For most people, however, this is a more affordable means of home construction than a traditional house.

Shipping containers are made of steel and will need to be wired for electricity, utilities will need to be installed, and insulation is incredibly important. Since they are made from steel, they conduct and retain heat incredibly well. This means that the inside of an uninsulated shipping container can reach extremely high temperatures. You will need to ensure that you have adequate insulation in your home, or it will be uninhabitable during the hottest parts of the year.

Being so conducive to heat transfer, shipping containers may also have an issue with excessive humidity, which, if not addressed, can lead to a host of major problems. To counter this, you will need to ensure the construction is well ventilated.

Many shipping containers come with wooden floors, which at first might seem great as this is an additional element that one doesn't have to buy. However, as nice as that would be, it isn't the case. The wood used in shipping containers is treated with a variety of chemicals and other potentially dangerous materials and will need to be removed before the construction process begins. It is highly advised that this is one of the first things removed before the start of construction.

Many people will utilize multiple containers in the construction of a home, and this will require welding and removal of parts of the walls within the containers. This will, naturally, reduce the strength and stability of the container, and you will need to take this reduced strength into consideration when planning the rest of the building.

It should also be noted that most shipping containers don't have a ton of top strength as they are meant to carry loads inside the container. Most containers cannot handle more than about 600 pounds of weight on top, which means you will need to provide enhanced support for the roof if you plan on adding a more traditional peaked roof to the construction. Some people use the top of the structure as a roof, and others prefer a sloped, more traditional roof as it provides for further insulation and can aid water runoff.

Chapter 2: Benefits of Shipping Container Homes

There are a variety of unique benefits that come with a shipping container home, making them an attractive option for certain types of people. Whether you are conscious of your ecological footprint, want a home that can easily be moved, or simply like the affordability of these types of houses, shipping container homes provide it all! While they, of course, come with their own downsides and complications, there are tons of benefits to these homes, which is why we are seeing such a boom in their popularity.

What follows is, of course, not an exhaustive list of their benefits, but some of the most commonly cited ones.

Unique Benefits of Container Homes

One of the most commonly cited benefits of container homes is their versatility and the fact that there is so much room for creativity in their design and construction. Since they work together in a similar way to Lego blocks, you can create structures of very different sizes and shapes much more easily than you can with traditional home construction. The ability to interlock different containers together and to stack them on top of each other opens up almost endless options for design and configuration.

As we have noted a number of times already, another benefit of shipping container construction is that they are often a lot more affordable to build than a traditional house. This is because they take less material to build, and this material can often be purchased at deep discounts, particularly if you are buying second-hand containers.

There will still be a number of materials and inputs required for the full construction of the home, but this will amount to far less than what is needed for a conventional build. You will still have to lease or purchase land for the home to be on, and depending on your site, you may have to run in utilities and other elements that aren't already there. For an average-sized family, a nice, large container home can be built for less than $50,000. This opens home ownership up to a much larger segment of the population than would otherwise be able to afford a home of their own.

Some people choose to cover the exposed sides of their container home and put on a traditional shaped roof, making it difficult to distinguish this type of home from a conventional construction, at least from the outside. Others, like to display the exposed steel container walls to the street, giving their home a unique look. Others still, like to do a combination of these, where one exposed section of container is displayed to create a feature wall of sorts.

Due to the nature of the container home, it is actually pretty easy to expand the home to accommodate the needs of the family. If, for example, you have a growing family and need an additional room or open space, it is pretty easy to make an affordable addition to allow your home to grow with your family. You can use shipping containers to create a multilevel home or even to build a loft area.

Another key benefit of a shipping container home is its strength and durability. It shouldn't be surprising that shipping containers are built very tough and solidly considering their purpose. They have to carry huge loads of goods across vast distances that span a range of different climatic environments, all while ensuring that the products get to their destination safely. This means the containers are built to very high standards and are incredibly durable.

Again, it is important to note that while these containers are very durable and incredibly tough, cutting the containers or removing walls to create the desired shape for the construction will reduce the structural integrity of the containers, and you may need to provide additional internal support.

A container home can be an ideal home style for people who are into do-it-yourself projects. While most people need to employ contractors and engineers, some people have the skill and knowhow to do much or all of the work themselves, and this can be a great project for a do-it-yourselfer.

Pests can be a huge problem with conventional houses, and insects like termites can do a lot of damage to wood constructions. Shipping container homes, since they are largely made from steel containers, don't have nearly as big of a problem with bugs and pests as a traditional home does. If you have wooden outer siding, you may still experience problems with termites or other pests, depending on the area you live in, but this is far less of an issue for container homeowners.

Since a container home is built from, well, shipping containers, which are meant to travel, many of these homes can rather easily be moved from one site to another. This means, like a mobile home, it is possible to transport the home from one site to another. The ability to take your home wherever you want to go and to have a dwelling that can come with you if, for example, you want to change jobs is incredibly unique to container and mobile homes.

To some, the environmental benefits are the key selling point for container homes. As we learn more about the global environment and our impact on it, many want to find ways that they can reduce their carbon footprint and reduce their burden on the planet. As a result, we have seen a dramatic rise in the popularity and abundance of green building efforts. Shipping container homes represent just one of many types of homes that can be built in a far more environmentally friendly way than traditional constructions.

The main reason for this is that the bulk of the home's structure can be made from recycled materials. These are materials that have been used for some other purpose (in this case, shipping, of course) that are then converted for use in a completely different context. This keeps unnecessary waste out of the waste stream and provides you with strong and durable materials to build a home from.

The tiny house movement has seen an increase in interest in container homes, and this makes sense since you get a lot of square footage for the low number of materials used in construction. People also love the ability to take a material that was used for a completely different purpose and give it a "retirement" as a home.

You need far fewer material inputs for this type of house, especially less wood and concrete. While you need far less concrete than in a typical construction, you will still need it for the foundation of the home, sidewalks, patios, or other surfaces you may wish to have.

If the home is well designed and properly insulated, a container home can be incredibly energy efficient as well. This allows you to maintain the home at comfortable temperatures in both summer and winter, without the use of an excessive amount of energy. Many people put solar panels on top of these constructions, making the home even more efficient and greener.

While these homes can be as large as you like, those with an environmental focus can thoughtfully build a house that is smaller than most homes but still serves the needs of its owners. Obviously, the smaller the home, the fewer materials will be used in the construction process, thus making it greener and more affordable. For this very reason, container homes have been growing in popularity among the minimalist community.

Since this type of home is conducive to life pretty much anywhere and can be converted into a solar home, this type of structure makes it easier and more affordable to live off the grid. There are many other ways you can enhance the "greenness" of your home, such as the use of composting bins, rain barrels to collect water that can be used to water plants or other vegetation, and, of course, general recycling.

Perks of Quick Building and Ease of Construction

One of the key perks of a container home is how quickly a quality home can be built. Typically, construction is an expensive, long, and laborious process. With container homes, so much of the structural material is already built, and so it doesn't take nearly as much time to build a container home. Depending on the size and complexity of the home, these can be built in as little as 8 weeks, which is about half the time you can expect typical home construction to take.

For most conventional homes, the process takes about 4-6 months, and that is if all goes well. Anyone who has ever worked on a home construction project knows this isn't all that likely.

As we noted above, since much of the materials are already in place and attached, most of the time spent on construction is spent putting the pieces in place and then subsidiary actions. These include things like laying a foundation, plumbing, wiring, and welding together multiple containers.

Another benefit that adds to the quickness with which a container home can be built is that it doesn't have to be built onsite. You have the option of fabricating the home at a different location and simply bringing the structure in and placing it on top of the foundation when it is complete. This may significantly reduce the cost and time it takes to have a container home fully built.

The amount of time we discuss above is on the assumption that you will be completing the entire project onsite. If you have the home built offsite and transported to the desired location, or if you choose to buy a prefabricated homemade by a home builder, it will take a lot less time since the home simply needs to be transported and attached to the foundation.

As we have discussed a number of times, this type of home can be a much easier build than a traditional home since many of the main structural elements are already present in the container itself. If properly welded, you don't even have to have any internal walls to bear or distribute the weight. If you choose to have them, it will simply be for aesthetic purposes.

You also don't have to have an external roof unless you want to. However, in places known for hot summers, having an external roof can make it far easier and more energy-efficient to keep the home at a more bearable temperature. Many people will also employ landscaping to provide protection from the sun to reduce their energy needs.

Chapter 3: Overview of the Building Process

In this chapter, we will take a close look at all the elements of the building process, the decisions you will need to make, the order to do them in, and more. This will give you a much better idea of how to go about planning for your shipping container building, how to stay within your preferred budget, as well as all the considerations you will need to make when developing your plan of action.

As with any building or construction process, things will go far more smoothly if you know what exactly the process entails. This chapter seeks to introduce you to the various elements you will need to consider when planning for your new home.

Even with a simpler type of construction like a shipping container home - which takes less time to build and fewer materials, there are still codes the home must meet and elements of the construction you will want to pay close attention to. Taking the time to plan your build meticulously can save you a lot of time, money, and stress in the long run.

Main Elements of Planning and Construction

There are a lot of decisions that have to be made, even if you are building a tiny home. Having a keen understanding of the things you will need to plan for will make the construction process far more seamless and will get you in your new home as soon as possible. We will not touch on codes or specific permits here, as there are chapters dedicated to these issues later in this book.

Before you worry about building permits or actual plans for design, you will want to consider the location that you wish to build. Have you researched potential sites to see if they allow for the construction of non-traditional buildings? Have you inquired about the price of the land and any utilities that may have been installed beforehand? These questions will not only affect your ability to build at said site, but they will also affect the cost of the construction.

Depending on your financial status, you may wish to purchase or lease the land. If you are leasing the land, you will need to make sure building a non-traditional home on the site is acceptable to the landowner. Once all your questions have been answered and you have the ideal plot of land picked out, take a quick look at the local and state building regulations to make sure you are able to build a shipping container home on the land before buying or leasing.

Construction Necessities

There are a number of elements in home building that really aren't optional, whether it be for health and safety or for the fact that without certain things, the home would be unbearable in terms of temperature. Some of these things may seem really basic, and they are, but if you fail to address them, your build will end up costing a lot more money, taking more time, and being an overall frustrating experience.

One of the biggest mistakes home builders make - whether building a traditional home or a container home - is failing to properly insulate their home. This will dramatically reduce the efficiency of your home, meaning it will take more energy to keep the home at a comfortable temperature. With a shipping container home, failure to properly insulate could make the home unbearably hot during the summer months, hard to heat in the wintertime, and will likely cause regular issues with humidity.

As we noted in an earlier chapter, shipping containers are made from steel, especially a type of steel called Corten steel. All steel is highly conducive to trapping heat, and it takes a long time for the heat to dissipate from this material. This means that without proper insulation, the inside of the house can quickly reach extreme temperatures.

Any home benefits from good insulation, but with a shipping container home, it is vital. There are different kinds of insulation you can choose from, but the most commonly used are spray-in insulation and panel insulation. Spray foam is used to create a protective barrier against the elements and will reduce moisture within the structure. While spray-in insulation works in most climates, it works best in climates that are wetter and colder.

Panel insulation is, as the name implies, made in panel form and can easily be installed in a shipping container home. This type of insulation will work best in hotter, drier climates, but like with the spray-in insulation, you can really use this in any environment.

A final note on insulation: don't forget to insulate under your home. The foundation is directly exposed to earth, and the use of an extra layer of insulation under the home will further enhance the efficiency of the home and reduce the chances of problems with moisture. If you are adding an external roof to the home, you might also consider putting insulation in there as well.

It is important that you take care when choosing any and all building materials. As the adage goes, you get what you pay for, and your home isn't really the best place to skimp. So, for example, not all used shipping containers are created equally. Some have been maintained better than others, and some have been used for the transport of material that makes their use in home construction a bit questionable.

While this goes for all materials you plan to use in the construction of your home, you need to make sure that any shipping containers you plan to use in the construction of your home are of the proper quality and are in good repair. In a later chapter, we will touch on the basics of how to purchase good shipping containers and where you might source these materials from.

It is still useful to note here that you will need to check used shipping containers very closely. Check for leaks, holes, cracks, or any signs of mold or moisture. Most importantly, you will want to check for signs of corrosion or rust, as this is like termites to a steel home. It is also worth noting that most people choose high cube containers to use in construction as they give an extra foot or so of headroom, which is useful for added vertical space, but this is really your choice.

Let's take a little aside to talk about rust, as this is something you will want to plan for in your build. Making sure the containers remain rust-free will be a large part of shipping container home ownership. While they are hardy and durable and resistant to many pests and elements, they are more at risk of rust and corrosion than traditional constructions since they are made from steel.

When new, shipping containers are often painted with anti-corrosion paint, which is very helpful but can also release noxious chemicals that are dangerous to your health. This is another reason why good insulation is so important as it will protect you from the outgassing. If you are purchasing a used container, it might be a good idea to put a fresh coat of anti-corrosion paint on the containers when you have finished your construction.

Whether you purchase a new container that has already been built, or you plan on painting the container yourself, you will want to check the container over for any chips or other areas that may need further repair. It is recommended to wait until you are done with the construction to repaint the container as it is too easy for the paint to be chipped during the building process.

Avoid having any bare metal exposed to the elements anywhere on the house, as this will make it more prone to rust and corrosion.

We will devote a chapter to permits as we noted earlier, and there we will also touch on zoning and other issues you will need to address when planning for the specifics of the build, but it doesn't hurt to mention that these will be required and it is helpful to know what to expect in advance to as to speed the process up. Not having a good plan of action will likely lead to delays, added costs, and general frustration. This is a good time to consider the spaces you will need and want in your new home and how to best plan your design around these needs.

Budgeting is also incredibly important. Not only is it helpful to know what you can afford to spend on each stage of the construction project, but it will help you stay on budget and not find yourself going over budget due to poor planning. Even though a container home is cheaper than a traditional home, it is still likely the biggest investment you will make, and it is where you will spend the bulk of your time. You need to plan a realistic budget that you can manage on your income, taking into account all the varied costs associated with a construction project.

Most people assume that once they have purchased the land, it is ready to build on once all permits are in place. This is a mistake, unless the land has already been graded and had utilities installed. If the land isn't improved at all at the time of purchase, you will need to do a number of things to prepare the land for construction. This is especially true for people building in rural areas.

Chances are, there will be some trees or other types of brush that will need to be removed from the property. Foundations are the first part of any home construction process, and they require flat and level land; otherwise, the resulting structure may not have the best integrity and might not pass inspection.

If you plan on having a driveway or patio or any other paved surface, you will also need to level the ground for this as well. It will also be important that your home have access to main roads. It is also important to think about the type of utilities you need installed on your land and start looking at trained professionals who might be able to provide their services for the project. Unless you have a ton of skill in the area of plumbing, electricity, or internet installation, chances are you will need to bring someone in to make sure the utilities are safely installed and meet local safety code.

We have touched on it a time or two, but here is where we should take a closer look at using architects and contractors to help in designing and building your home. If you are a skilled do-it-yourselfer, there is a good chance that there are numerous elements of building a shipping container home that you can easily manage yourself. However, even if you are skilled in construction, chances are you don't know how to do everything required in building a shipping container home and thus may need assistance.

If you have little or no building experience, you will obviously need to employ the help of trained professionals. There are now companies that specialize in the design or building of shipping container homes, but this is still a niche type of construction, and the direct experience may not be available in your area. There is no problem with hiring traditional home building contractors to take on this type of project since most of the construction will be elements they are well versed with.

You should make sure that any contractor you consider has someone on staff that has welding experience, as this is something that will be needed to fasten multiple shipping containers together and to make a multi-level home.

When choosing a contractor, obviously, price is important, but there are other factors that are more so. Reputation and the quality of the experience of a given contractor or company are vital. You want to make sure that the people you are hiring to build your home do good work, are reliable, stick to the budget, and follow through on their promises. You will need to do a little research. The internet is a great place to start, but it is also helpful to ask around and get some feedback from people who have actually used the contractor so you can be sure you are choosing a quality worker.

Since contractors aren't the only expertise you may require for the build, this is also a good time to research plumbers, electricians, architects, and anyone else who might provide needed assistance during the build.

If you are hiring an architect or designer to create plans for your home, you should find a few potential options and check out what they have to offer. You can be very specific about what you are looking for, what you need, what you plan to use spaces for, and any aesthetic preferences you might have.

The first thing that you will need to look into are the zoning laws in your local area. Zoning laws determine what types of buildings and businesses can be built where. This is why you don't often find industrial factories right next to neighborhoods. Some places have more mixed zoning, for example, allowing small amounts of commercial development near residential areas, but this will vary from town to town and state to state.

Other homeowners in traditionally residential areas may not want a shipping container home in their neighborhood and may even lobby the local government or building association to keep the neighborhood free of any non-traditional construction. Many fear (unnecessarily) that this type of non-traditional construction will lower the value of the houses in the area since they look so different. It is vital that you make sure that any potential land or area you want to build in doesn't have rules against non-traditional constructions, as you may not be able to build there.

You will need to get in touch with the local building authorities to have any plans or blueprints checked to make sure they meet the correct codes and that it is possible for you to build a non-traditional home in the desired location. It can be really helpful to start by researching the local and state rules relating to non-traditional home construction as this will give you a better idea of what types of permits you will need to obtain, where you can build, and the types of code that you will need to make sure the construction meets.

While researching non-traditional construction rules and regulations can be very helpful, it is important to note that there still may be some additional rules or requirements in your local area for shipping container homes. For this, make sure you get in touch with local building authorities to check on rules specifically relating to shipping container homes.

More rural or remote areas are more likely to have friendlier rules surrounding the construction of this type of home than an urban area. Texas, Louisiana, California, Tennessee, Missouri, Oregon, and Alaska have some of the friendliest rules for the building of non-traditional and shipping container homes. There are more areas in these states where you are allowed to build this type of home, and the rules are not as prohibitive as they are in other states. This isn't to say that shipping container homes aren't suitable in other states; they just have stricter requirements for their construction and tighter rules on where these constructions can be built.

We have noted a couple of times that rural or remote areas tend to have the friendliest rules for the construction of non-traditional homes, and this is true even in states that have relaxed rules surrounding non-traditional construction to begin with. Urban and suburban areas have much more stringent rules, and urban areas simply have far less available space, which is part of why it is more difficult to obtain land and the proper permits to build in these areas. That doesn't mean there aren't urban or suburban places that you can build these types of homes; it is just pretty rare.

In almost every state, a construction project will require obtaining a building permit. The basic reason for this requirement is to ensure that any new constructions are built to specific occupancy and safety standards, are built with acceptable materials, and have certain basic elements like proper plumbing and electricity installed.

Obtaining a Building Permit

Regardless of where you build - and whether it is in a rural or urban area - you will be required to obtain a building permit in order to legally begin construction of your home. You can face stiff fines and other penalties if you try to avoid this part of the process or fail to follow the proper protocol for application.

Though it might seem like an unnecessary extra step, building permits exist for a good reason. They help ensure that all new constructions meet basic safety standards, are designed properly, and meet residential building code that is set at an international and local level.

There are a few things you will need to do before you even apply for the building permit. First, you will need to prepare comprehensive site plans, such as building designs or blueprints. For more extensive projects or in areas that have more stringent building codes, it is often easier to hire an architect or other trained builder who has an in-depth understanding of what is required to obtain a building permit, as this will help ensure you don't overlook anything major that might result in the denial of your application.

Depending on your location, the actual process of applying may vary. Most states and localities require a pre-approval process where your initial plans are looked over and either approved or sent back with changes that need to be made in order for the project to meet the requirements. This process can go pretty quickly, or it can take a number of weeks, depending on where you live. If you have to make changes or revisions to your project, this will obviously mean that it will take longer to obtain a permit.

The most common reasons an application will need revision is a failure to comply with basic building codes. We discuss the basics of these codes below, and it is important that your plans and blueprints address all commonly required building codes like fire safety, sanitation, ventilation, and so on.

Just because you need to make revisions to your project doesn't mean that you won't be approved for a building permit. Local officials are often very helpful in providing advice on making changes that will help you meet international and local codes. Again, with the help of an architect or other experienced professional, you can avoid these mistakes to begin with.

The more detailed information you can provide, the easier it is to get approved for a building permit. It is important to remember that a city official must interpret your ability to adhere to code based on the material you give them. There will also be fees associated with this process, and you should be prepared for this.

You must have an approved permit before you can begin any part of the construction process. Even though it is hard to wait and can be tempting to get started on some basic parts of the project, it can jeopardize your ability to successfully obtain a permit. It could also result in fines.

The permit review process will address zoning codes, safety codes, environmental regulation, codes relating to utilities and plumbing, as well as the basic dimensions of the building structure. Making sure you provide detailed and thorough documentation also helps this process go a lot faster as well, but it is important to note that even with the best plans, this type of process takes time, so you should plan for that and not think that you can immediately start construction once your application is submitted.

Some states and localities have further fees associated with obtaining a building permit, and these should be clearly laid out on your local building authority's website or on any literature they provide in person. You will get a permit, as well as a job inspection card that inspectors will stamp after an inspection has been completed. You will also be given a set of state stamped documents showing your approval for the construction process.

Once you have a permit, you can begin construction, but this isn't the end of making sure you comply with the permit requirements and local building codes and regulations. Chances are, at a few different points in the construction process, you will need to have someone to come inspect your progress and how the building is being constructed to comply with the city's rules.

When the construction process is complete, you will need to have a final inspection of the property. This is where your project will be marked as meeting zoning compliance, utility compliance, and occupancy compliance.

If you have met all codes and requirements, the city will sign off and give final approval for the project, and you are good to go with moving in and putting any finishing touches on the project.

Residential Codes

Whether you are building a shipping container home or traditional construction, a dwelling that is only intended as a living space must be built in a residential area. There are different rules surrounding places of business that have homes built on top or otherwise attached to them, and this also applies to both shipping container homes and traditional types of construction.

The codes and rules surrounding plumbing and electricity will be similar whether you are building a container home or a traditional one. The energy codes in your state will be based on the International Energy Conservation Code. Different states abide by different codes, but they are all based on this international body's standards.

Codes that relate to safety are pretty much uniform across all states and will apply to any type of residential construction, whether traditional or non-traditional. One of the most important safety codes you will have to follow relates to exits and emergency escapes. There must be one operable window or door in every sleeping room in the home, and it must access a public street or open space. This is largely for fire safety but can be useful for other types of emergencies as well.

Other basic building codes relate to lighting, ventilation, and sanitation. Exterior openings such as windows or skylights are required to provide a minimum amount of natural light into the structure. There are exceptions that can be made for the installation of a roofed porch or patio in place of windows at the front or back of the home. Kitchens are an exception to the window rule so long as they have artificial lighting.

Ceilings must be no less than 7 feet tall in hallways and 7" 6' in any rooms designed for living. Also, rooms need to be about 65% open and not blocked by cabinetry or appliances. These open spaces will help allow for better ventilation and to ensure the safety of the internal structure for habitation.

Some states also have requirements for the minimum size of grassed yards or paved courtyard spaces, which can vary based on the locality.

For sanitation purposes, all dwellings will need to have a bathroom, kitchen sink, and access to both hot and cold water. You will also need adequate plumbing that allows for the removal of waste via a sewer system or a septic tank. Rural areas may have different requirements.

There are rules and codes related to the size and dimensions of rooms allowed within a residential structure. Most areas require that a residential structure contain at least 120 square feet of living space.

All residential dwellings must have smoke detectors, and, depending on your locality and the size of the property, you may need to have a sprinkler system as well.

For areas that experience winter or cold weather, you must have a heater to ensure the home can be maintained at a proper temperature.

If you want to have a garage on your home, there are also codes that relate to their construction. Regulations will determine the size and types of materials that may be used for the construction of a garage, whether attached to the home or an unattached unit.

For a multilevel construction, there are rules relating to stairways. They need to be no less than 36" wide, and steps should be at least 4" in height. If you want to use winding, circular, or spiral staircases, you will need to look at the specific requirements for these in your area.

If you have 4 or fewer steps leading to the next level, you aren't required to have a handrail. However, if they are of 30" in height or more, a handrail will need to be installed on at least one side. Those that are taller than 44 inches may require handrails on both sides, but you should check with your local building authorities for the specifics about handrails. If the stairs are open on one or both sides, it will need a hand or guardrail regardless of height.

These are some of the most common and basic residential building codes that you will have to adhere to when building a shipping container home. There may be more rules in your local area depending on what set of coding standards your state and locality adheres to. It is important to have a clear understanding of the specific requirements in your locality and state to make sure you don't miss something important.

Depending on the size and occupancy level of your structure, you may be able to get around some of these codes that are more designed for homes that have high levels of occupancy, but again, you will need to contact your local building authorities to find out about specific rules applying to your area.

While all of these codes can seem daunting, they can easily be adhered to by hiring an experienced builder or architect who will be familiar with the requirements of your local area.

Chapter 5: How to Plan for a Container Home Build

Just like any home construction project, building a container home requires paying attention to detail if you wish for the process to go forth efficiently and without issues. While these projects tend to be simpler than traditional home construction, there are still considerations you will need to address and basic planning that needs to be done before the building process actually begins.

Failure to have a good plan of action can lead to tons of unforeseen problems and could even lead to serious issues in the construction of your home. Though you can't, of course, plan for every aspect of a build and unforeseen things will likely happen even with good plans, you will have far fewer issues if you have a basic idea of how to address each step of the process. It is always better to be prepared.

Major Elements of the Build

The very first thing you will want to do when planning your container home construction is to set a budget. This is highly important as otherwise, costs can quickly spiral out of control, and nobody wants to be stuck with a partially finished home and lack the money to finish up the building project. With a budget, you can more easily see where your money goes and where you might end up going over budget, so it doesn't end up being an unpleasant surprise.

Most recommend that you have a contingency fund in your budget as well. This is a percentage of money that can be used for unforeseen costs and things that may run over budget. This is just something that happens with home building, and it is better to be prepared and already have funds set aside than scrambling at the last minute to try to figure out where to get extra funds for your project. Experts recommend setting aside an extra 20% of the amount you have budgeted to allow for unforeseen costs. If all goes well, this is money that you simply don't have to spend, and unexpected savings are always a perk, too!

Once you have your budget set, you will want to start scouting out potential plots of land or lots that are already divided. Some lots will already have utilities installed, which will likely add to the cost of buying the plot, but it does save time and effort in the building process. If you are buying land in a more remote or rural area, you are likely going to have to put in all the utilities needed for your home. It isn't recommended that you purchase land without first seeing it in person. You want to make sure the land is as described, and seeing it in person will allow you to have a better idea of where to place your construction, as well as ideas for landscaping, sidewalks, driveways, and the like.

Before you purchase any land, you will want to look into permits and regulations in your area. Every locality is different, and there will be widely varied rules relating to the construction and code for building shipping container homes. Though a lot rarer nowadays, there are still some places where you just simply can't build a container home, and you don't want to find this out after you've purchased land.

Make sure you have everything you will need when it comes to getting a building permit and that you have a good understanding of the local and state regulations and codes surrounding residential constructions, and especially those that apply to mobile homes and non-traditional structures.

Next, you will want to consider home designs. You may want to design your home yourself, have an architect design it, or you can even find fully-fledged designs online that tell you all the materials you need and layout a detailed floor plan. Once you have a few options narrowed down, you will want to take it to an architect or engineer to determine which plan is best for the land you wish to build on. They have the expertise to know what you may not have considered when looking at designs.

You will also want to think about who will build your home. Are you going to do it all yourself? Do you have all the skills, tools, and know-how to make that happen? It is important to be honest with yourself about your building abilities. You can run into real trouble if part way through a build, you realize that you don't know how to do part of the project. Will you have architects or contractors working on your home build? Not only will the answers to these questions affect the cost of the build, but this is also where you need to start researching people in your area to find reputable and available people who can do the job.

A note about contractors: a good contractor with a lot of welding experience will be able to minimize the amount of welding that needs to be done on your container home. Remember that the more welding that is done, the less structural integrity the containers retain, and this can necessitate additional support, which will further add to the cost and could cut down on usable floor space.

When planning your build, you will also want to take into account the local climatic conditions of your area. Is there a ton of wind and rain? Are the summers particularly hot? The answers to these questions will help determine the orientation of the house and can also necessitate things like additional insulation. You will also need to consider any type of landscaping or terraforming that may need to be done to level out the ground for a foundation, driveway, patio, etc.

Will you need to run all or some of the utilities to the land you want to build on? You will need to make sure you know what all is entailed and get in touch with a quality plumber and electrician ahead of time so they can come out and look at your land and give you a good estimate on cost and the amount of time it will take to finish the install.

Obviously, you will also need to source your building materials, which in this case, will largely mean shipping containers. You need to visit and purchase the correct number of containers and figure out how to have them transported to the site. It is vital that you purchase the correct number of shipping containers as it can really slow down the process and add to the cost to have to stop and wait for another shipping container to arrive. It is recommend to obtain the necessary permits before investing in the containers.

As we noted earlier, many shipping containers have wood floors already installed. This wood is treated with a range of chemicals that are dangerous or potentially harmful to people and animals and will need to be removed. If the container has been treated with paint to resist corrosion, there is a good chance that this paint can outgas potentially dangerous compounds. It is important to properly strip this paint and remove the wooden boards prior to beginning your build.

Finally, you will want to plan your interior design. This means sourcing cabinets and fixtures, as well as paint, flooring, and the like.

Chapter 6: How to Source a Shipping Container

Purchasing shipping containers might seem like it would be the easiest part of the process, but this, too, will require some research and a bit of homework. Remember, these containers are an investment and will comprise the main bulk of your home. You don't want to just pick any old container as you can end up with containers in ill repair or that simply aren't suitable for use in home construction.

Many people are at a loss as to where to find shipping containers for sale but may be surprised to find out that they can be purchased from a wide variety of different places, locally, nationally, and even internationally. However, if you are purchasing shipping containers internationally, you should be prepared for much higher transportation costs than if you source your containers from within your own country or locality.

Simply finding a good deal on shipping containers is where the work begins, not ends. You need to make sure the containers are as promised. You need to make sure they are the right size for your needs and that they are in good shape. There are certain types of shipping containers, such as one-way use, or as are containers that aren't great for building, and this should be taken into consideration when looking at potential containers.

Buying new containers will, of course, be more expensive than buying used containers, but they are guaranteed to be in better repair and will not have any travel damage or wear and tear on them. Used shipping containers are highly suitable for building if they are well maintained and don't have any holes or leaks in them. It is important that you know what any used shipping container shipped while in use as it may require some extra work to get out any chemicals that could be potentially harmful.

Buying Containers

As we noted above, shipping containers can be purchased, new or used, from a variety of companies local, national, and international. There are even some completely online sellers. However, it is not recommended that you buy containers sight unseen. Not only are they an investment, they will literally be your home, and you don't want to take the risk of receiving poorly maintained containers.

Even if you are working with a local or national dealer, chances are that much of the process will take place online. That is just the nature of modern business. But this means that you will need to do your homework. Make sure any potential container supplier has a good reputation and a time-honored history of providing good service and value. While it might be tempting to simply go with the cheapest option, you often get what you pay for, as the old adage goes, and you can get burned in the process if you don't practice due diligence.

You want to consider the reputation of the supplier. Check out customer reviews and, if possible, talk to people who have done business with them and gauge their experience as well as their opinion on the quality of the materials and services offered. Of course, the price will be a factor, and it only makes financial sense to work with a supplier that has competitive and reasonable prices. A local supplier may not have the economies of scale to offer the lowest prices, but they may have value-added services that make up for any difference in price.

Though it is not the case with all shipping container suppliers, some new and used container purveyors will have money-back guarantees and even warranties on their products. This gives added peace of mind and is perhaps something you want to look for in a supplier. Make sure you carefully read and understand what the warranty entails, so you aren't caught off guard, thinking it covers "x" when it does not.

With any potential supplier, you will want to find out about the delivery process. Does the company offer delivery of shipping containers? If so, is this an additional cost? If they do provide delivery, do they offload the containers too, or will this be your responsibility? If shipping is not included, you will need to make sure that you have access to what is needed to move the containers.

For standard, smaller containers, a forklift and a truck will likely be all you need for transport. Larger containers and high cube containers may require the use of a crane or other equipment designed for moving heavy and large material. You will need to ensure that you can obtain or hire someone who has this equipment as shipping containers aren't much use if you can't get them where they need to be.

When it comes to inspecting potential containers, there are a number of things that you will want to look for and questions to ask. One of the most important questions is to find out what the container was used to ship. The dealer might not know exactly, but they should know if the containers were used to transport hazardous materials or not. A container designed to transport hazardous materials isn't necessarily unsuitable for building, but you will need to make sure you can get the container properly cleaned before any construction begins.

You will want to check for any sort of damage to the containers, including leaks, holes, rust or corrosion, and evidence of chemical damage. It is also important to look at the roof. While it may not seem important, it really is. Dents in the roof can trap water, which can lead to rust or corrosion, which is can be a huge problem for the structural integrity of the home.

Websites like BoxHub can be found with a simple internet search. BoxHub specifically is a well-known and trusted supplier of shipping containers to customers across the United States. They have a wide selection of containers of different sizes, making them one of the best places to go if you want a wide selection of options. The economies of scale of this company mean that they can offer competitive prices that are often lower than other sellers. They offer a money-back guarantee and provide at-cost delivery options.

If BoxHub isn't for you or doesn't have what you want, a basic web search will point you to a number of potential suppliers that serve your local area or nationwide. There are smaller places that, for whatever reason, may have shipping containers simply sitting around, taking up space on their lots, even if selling shipping containers isn't their main business. You might be able to find really good deals at places like this, but you will really want to inspect the containers before purchase and will likely have to manage the transportation yourself.

Financial Considerations

While building a shipping container home can be much cheaper than homes of traditional construction, the materials are still an investment, and so it makes sense to do your homework. Not only will this make sure you don't break the bank in the construction process, but it will also help ensure that you end up with a high-quality home that will meet your needs and expectations.

Shipping containers range in cost from about $500-4000, depending on the size and quality of the container. They can be paid for outright with cash or check, you can use a credit card to purchase it, or you may even be able to finance the containers at the dealer. Financing can be a great option if you are buying a large number of containers. It also works to inquire about any discounts for larger purchases as some places will reduce their prices if you buy a certain number of containers.

You will want to consider any warranties and the return process when deciding where to buy containers from. Warranties provide peace of mind that you are covered if anything happens to your shipping containers. These may come with the purchase or may need to be purchased separately. Make sure you understand the terms of the warranty before making a purchase. You will also want to know about their process for returns. While this doesn't happen often, you could find an issue with a container once it has been delivered, and you want to make sure the company has policies in place for addressing any issues that might be found after purchase.

It is also worthwhile to consider any value-added services the company may offer. This includes things like repairing or cleaning the containers before transport, or the removal of wooden floors. Some companies will offer transport, delivery, or offloading services for a fee. Unless you have an easy way to get the containers from point A to point B, this will be important and is likely to come with an additional cost.

Chapter 7: How to Manage a Container Home Build

Managing any type of construction project can be a time-consuming and difficult endeavor, but with some understanding of what is involved, it can make this process at least a little easier. Good planning and some research ahead of time can really streamline this process and help reduce as many problems as possible. Of course, you can't plan for every contingency, and there is still a chance that something unforeseen will arise, but with good planning and an understanding of the basic steps of the building process, you will be much more prepared.

What follows is the basic plan of action that you will need to follow to ensure that you are properly prepared for the building process and all that goes with it. It isn't, of course, an exhaustive list, but it gives you the information you need to develop a good plan for what you need to do and what type of oversight you may need to provide.

First Steps

Though it can be tempting to jump into home design and all the fun considerations that go along with it, there are some other things you will need to address before you get started. The first thing you will need to do is locate potential pieces of property where you might want to build your container home. This not only means looking at actual plots of land but also looking into local codes and permits requirements to ensure that you can actually build what you want in the location you are considering.

Once you have determined that you can build a shipping container home on the said plot of land and you understand the codes and regulations surrounding the build, you will want to purchase the land. This could mean simply purchasing it outright, or you may be financing the land as part of a mortgage or other type of loan.

After you have taken care of purchasing the land, you will need to make a detailed survey of the land. You may be able to do this yourself, or you may prefer to have a surveyor come out and do this. With this survey of your land, you can begin to create comprehensive blueprints and building plans as this will not only help in the building process, but is also going to be imperative when applying for building permits and meeting local and state code.

Many people hire a professional architect or engineer for this part of the process since they have more experience and in-depth knowledge of local rules and thus may be able to spot any potential issues with your construction plans. Structural engineers can look over or develop plans that will meet the codes and regulations of your local area.

After you've obtained the land, had it surveyed, and created detailed plans for the build, it is time to obtain a building permit and any other permits that might be required for new construction in your area.

When you have all the required permits, you will need to source all your building materials. This means, of course, shipping containers, but you will also need concrete, drywall, and roofing materials as well. It is a good idea to have a really detailed list of all the supplies you need, as this makes acquiring them far easier. If you hired a contractor, they could often source the materials themselves, and this will be added to the cost of their services.

Preparing the Land and the Actual Build

You will need to prepare your land for laying a foundation, which doesn't seem like it entails much, but it really depends on the terrain you are building on. The underlying substructure of the soil must be strong enough to hold the weight of the construction, and the land needs to be flat and at a stable grade before the foundation is poured. You will also want to consider any land that will be used for driveways, sidewalks, patios, etc., and make sure the land is level and suitable for construction.

It is important that your foundation, whether you choose to have it built of concrete or wood, is properly reinforced so it can handle the weight of the house and doesn't crack with temperature changes through the seasons. Once the foundation has been laid, you will need to give it the proper amount of time to cure and set before putting any weight on top of it.

This is a great time to bring in utilities before the main part of the construction begins. You will likely need a plumbing expert and an electrician to ensure that the utilities are safely and properly installed on the property.

After these basic elements are in place, you will begin building the structure itself. When the structural elements are brought in, they will be anchored to the foundation, usually attached to all four sides of the foundation.

Once the main parts of the structure are in place, you need to properly insulate the structure. It is advised that you insulate under the home, and if you plan on having an external roof, you might consider putting extra insulation in there as well, as this will help to improve the efficiency of your home.

After the insulation is installed, wiring and plumbing, exterior siding, and external roofs, you will want to install interior walls, windows, doors, and floors. Finally, any cabinetry or other fixtures in the home will need to be installed. Once this is complete, you just need to add any finishing touches you wish to the interior, and the landscape.

Chapter 8: Unique Design Ideas

So, you might be thinking, this is all well and good, and we've gotten deep into the proverbial meat and potatoes of building a shipping container home and everything that it will entail, but are we ever going to look closer at design? Never fear, last but not least, in our handy guide, we are going to touch on designing your home.

We have mentioned numerous times that designing a shipping container house allows for far greater creativity in design than most other types of construction. This means you can let your imagination run wild as cost and space are likely to be the most prohibitive issues in design. Think about how you use space, what kind of aesthetics you prefer, what type of floor plan will work best for you and your family. These factors will all help guide you in the development of a basic design for your new home.

If you design your own home, it is still recommended that you run your plans or blueprints by a structural engineer or architect. They will be able to provide feedback about any changes you might need to make to ensure your structure is stable and safe.

But let's say you aren't a designer and have no idea what you want your home to look like. Well, in this case, you have two major options: going to an architect directly or purchasing already made design plans online.

Architects and Online Designs

Going to an architect to help you create a design for your home will give you the peace of mind that you are going to get a solid design that meets both safety guidelines, and your needs. However, you should be prepared that this will come at an additional cost, and it may take a while for them to come up with a design that works for you. If you have really clear ideas as to how you want the home laid out and what design elements are important to you, this might be a good option.

Other options are to find blueprints and floor plans online. There are numerous sites that have a range of different floor plans for sale, from tiny homes to multi-level buildings that have both commercial and living space. Many of these homes are designed to maximize the usable floor space with as few containers and building materials as possible. Others are meant to be large, lavish homes that have a ton of open floor space, windows, and even multiple levels.

Many of these designs will come with information about what you will need to purchase in order to build the design, including the number and type of shipping containers used in construction.

This is a great way to get access to a huge range of different styles in case you aren't exactly sure what you are looking for or what kind of design will best suit you. These designs will all have basic elements like a living space, bedrooms, kitchens, and bathrooms, but will vary in size and sophistication. For many, this is a far more affordable way to access quality designs for their home.

A Brief Look at Some Popular Designs

There are tons of great designs online, and here we will touch on three different styles. While these are great designs, don't feel limited by just these designs as there are countless places online to find really interesting and unique blueprints.

One of the most popular designs available online is the Honomobo H4. This is a 700 square foot home that features two bedrooms, a kitchen, bathroom, and a living room. It is one of the most efficient container homes you can find online. It's has an open floor plan, and a long glass wall provides for maximum use of space as well as an airy feel. This construction of this home requires four 40-foot containers.

The SunDog Structures Live/Work 2070 is a really unique design that is a larger, multi-level construction. The home has 2,070 square feet, and the lower level is designed so it can be used as a commercial or other working space, with the traditional living space on the second level. The lower floor has a completely open floor plan and can be designed with a glass front to make it usable as a storefront. The upper floor has two bedrooms, two bathrooms, a kitchen, and a large living room space. This design requires seven 40-foot, high cube containers for construction.

Finally, we have the small but remarkably roomy Luckdrops Studio +. This is a one-bedroom, one-bathroom container home that consists of 287 square feet. While this is much smaller than the other two premade designs, it has quite a bit of usable floor space and makes a great home for a single individual or couple. The home also features a galley, space-saving kitchen, an L-shaped living room space, and a bathroom at the end of the building. It is made from two 40 ft containers and is one of the most affordable to build. The construction of this home can be completed for less than $40,000.

Conclusion

Shipping container homes are a unique type of home construction that have a ton of different benefits. They are versatile creations that can be built in any number of configurations, which leaves a lot of room open for creativity and innovative design. Some container homes take on the appearance of a traditional home, whereas others are true feats of design, looking like a Jenga puzzle, with elements jutting out in all directions. The proverbial sky really is the limit when it comes to what can be done design-wise with container homes.

Since shipping containers are designed for heavy-duty use, they are often incredibly well built and resistant to a variety of elements, from wind and rain to certain substances like salt. They are built in standard sizes and are designed to interlock with other containers during travel, which makes combining multiple containers together in construction incredibly simple, even enhancing the strength of the construction.

These shipping containers may only be available in two standard sizes, but they can be combined in a ton of different ways to create a unique and open floor plan that can meet the needs of even a large family. Multiple containers can be interlocked together, stacked on top of each other, and containers can even have walls or other parts removed to enhance floor space, or to give a room a unique shape and feel.

There are millions of unused shipping containers, essentially collecting dust and taking up space, which could easily be converted into functional living and working spaces. With so many already available, this abundant material can be purchased for a fraction of the cost of new containers, and for far less money than traditional building materials. A well-maintained shipping container makes a great construction material while also removing waste from our overburdened waste stream, in essence, recycling what was trash into a completely new building.

Being able to make a home from recycled materials is becoming more popular and desirable as more people are developing greater environmental consciousness. These homes can be built in incredibly remote areas and are conducive to the installation of solar panels, making them an excellent option for people who want to build a home off-the-grid.

In addition to being more environmentally friendly, shipping container homes, especially when made from used containers and a simple design, are often a lot more affordable than a traditional home, opening home ownership up to a much larger swath of the population. As rent prices continue to soar, and the cost of buying a home gets further from many people's reach, alternative means of construction like container homes are becoming a lot more attractive to many people.

They are also popular for their versatility and ability to be moved. Whether prefabricated or constructed onsite, since these dwellings are made from containers that are designed to be shipped, many container homes can easily be moved from one site to another. This means that even if you want to move to an entirely new state or even country, you may be able to literally take your home with you.

There are many reasons that homes constructed from shipping containers are growing in popularity, including cost efficiency, adaptability, and environmentally friendly designs. Whatever the reason for your interest in shipping container homes, you should now be armed with the information you need to approach the building process in a thoughtful and carefully planned way.

I hope you have enjoyed this book and found it to be helpful. I wish you the best of luck on your journey into the world of shipping container home construction!

www.ingramcontent.com/pod-product-compliance
Lightning Source LLC
LaVergne TN
LVHW021735060526
838200LV00052B/3291